Come, Follow Me

This journal belongs to:

_____

2019 is an exciting time to be a member of the Church of Jesus Christ of Latter-day Saints. In the October 2018 General Conference of the Church President Russell M. Nelson announced a fundamental change in the way we worship. Pres. Nelson stated, "It is time for a home-centered Church, supported by what takes place inside our branch, ward, and stake buildings." Members of the Church of Jesus Christ are now invited to take part in "a home-centered and Church-supported plan to learn doctrine, strengthen faith, and foster greater personal worship."

This journal supports your personal or family home-centered plan for gospel learning and worship. In conjunction with *Come, Follow Me—For Individuals and Families*, weekly gospel study topics are listed. These home study topics coordinate with the *Come, Follow Me* lessons that classes and quorums will study in Sunday meetings.

Each week lists the scriptures and topics to study. This is a guide, but not a hard and fast rule. As it states in *Come, Follow Me—For Individuals and Families*, "The schedule will help you keep up with the material covered in Sunday classes, but don't feel bound by it; the schedule is simply a guide to help you pace yourself. The important thing is that you are learning the gospel individually and as a family."

Along the bottom of each week's pages are study aids and prompts you can ponder as you study. These ideas are provided to help you improve your personal or family scripture study, but are just a sampling of the many things you can focus on. You can take notes, record impressions, doodle scenes from the scriptures, or anything else you feel inspired to do. Each week's pages are left open so you have the freedom to use them as you want.

As we study the scriptures together and seek for a deeper conversion we will be able to strengthen our homes, our families, and our wards and stakes. As Elder Quintin L. Cook taught, "We know the spiritual impact and the deep and lasting conversion that can be achieved in the home setting…. We are confident that members will be blessed in extraordinary ways. Sunday can be a day of gospel learning and teaching at church and in the home. As individuals and families engage in family councils, family history, ministering, service, personal worship, and joyful family time, the Sabbath day will truly be a delight."

Come, Follow Me

Weekly Study Chart

- ○ 12/31-01/06   We Are Responsible for Our Own Learning
- ○ 01/07-01/13   Matthew 1; Luke 1
- ○ 01/14-01/20   Luke 2; Matthew 2
- ○ 01/21-01/27   John 1
- ○ 01/28-02/03   Matthew 3; Mark 1; Luke 3
- ○ 02/04-02/10   Matthew 4; Luke 4-5
- ○ 02/11-02/17   John 2-4
- ○ 02/18-02/24   Matthew 5; Luke 6
- ○ 02/25-03/03   Matthew 6-7
- ○ 03/04-03/10   Matthew 8-9; Mark 2-5
- ○ 03/11-03/17   Matthew 10-12; Mark 2; Luke 7; 11
- ○ 03/18-03/24   Matthew 13; Luke 8; 13
- ○ 03/25-03/31   Matthew 14-15; Mark 6-7; John 5-6
- ○ 04/01-04/14   Matthew 16-17; Mark 9; Luke 9
- ○ 04/15-04/21   Easter
- ○ 04/22-04/28   Matthew 18; Luke 10
- ○ 04/29-05/05   John 7-10
- ○ 05/06-05/12   Luke 12-17; John 11
- ○ 05/13-05/19   Matthew 19-20; Mark 10; Luke 18
- ○ 05/20-05/26   Matthew 21-23; Mark 11; Luke 19-20; John 12
- ○ 05/27-06/02   Joseph Smith—Matthew 1; Matthew 25; Mark 12-13; Luke 21
- ○ 06/03-06/09   John 13-17
- ○ 06/10-06/16   Matthew 26; Mark 14; Luke 22; John 18
- ○ 06/17-06/23   Matthew 27; Mark 15; Luke 23; John 19
- ○ 06/24-06/30   Matthew 28; Mark 16; Luke 24; John 20-21

Come, Follow Me

Weekly Study Chart

- ○ 07/01-07/07   Acts 1-5
- ○ 07/08-07/14   Acts 6-9
- ○ 07/15-07/21   Acts 10-15
- ○ 07/22-07/28   Acts 16-21
- ○ 07/29-08/04   Acts 22-28
- ○ 08/05-08/11   Romans 1-6
- ○ 08/12-08/18   Romans 7-16
- ○ 08/19-08/25   1 Corinthians 1-7
- ○ 08/26-09/01   1 Corinthians 8-13
- ○ 09/02-09/08   1 Corinthians 14-16
- ○ 09/09-09/15   2 Corinthians 1-7
- ○ 09/16-09/22   2 Corinthians 8-13
- ○ 09/23-09/29   Galatians
- ○ 09/30-10/13   Ephesians
- ○ 10/14-10/20   Philippians; Colossians
- ○ 10/21-10/27   1 and 2 Thessalonians
- ○ 10/28-11/03   1 and 2 Timothy; Titus; Philemon
- ○ 11/04-11/10   Hebrews 1-6
- ○ 11/11-11/17   Hebrews 7-13
- ○ 11/18-11/24   James
- ○ 11/25-12/01   1 and 2 Peter
- ○ 12/02-12/08   1-3 John; Jude
- ○ 12/09-12/15   Revelation 1-11
- ○ 12/16-12/22   Christmas
- ○ 12/23-12/29   Revelation 12-22

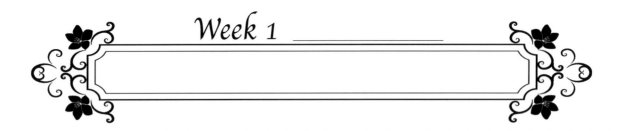

Week 1

We are Responsible for Our Own Learning

Ideas to Improve Your Personal Scripture Study

♪ Look for Truths about Jesus Christ
♪ Look for Inspiring Words and Phrases
♪ Liken the Scriptures to Your life
♪ Ask Questions as You Study
♪ Record Your Thoughts and Feelings

♪ Look for Gospel Truths
♪ Listen to the Spirit
♪ Use Scripture Study Helps
♪ Share Insights
♪ Live by What You Learn

♪ Study the Words of Latter-day Prophets and Apostles

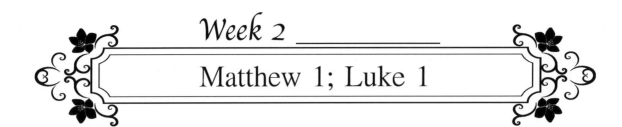

Ideas to Improve Your Personal Scripture Study

♪ Look for Truths about Jesus Christ ♪ Look for Gospel Truths

♪ Look for Inspiring Words and Phrases ♪ Listen to the Spirit

♪ Liken the Scriptures to Your life ♪ Use Scripture Study Helps

♪ Ask Questions as You Study ♪ Share Insights

♪ Record Your Thoughts and Feelings ♪ Live by What You Learn

♪ Study the Words of Latter-day Prophets and Apostles

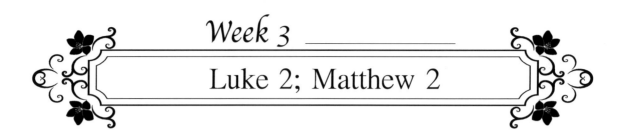

We Have Come to Worship Him

Ideas to Improve Your Personal Scripture Study

♪ Look for Truths about Jesus Christ
♪ Look for Inspiring Words and Phrases
♪ Liken the Scriptures to Your life
♪ Ask Questions as You Study
♪ Record Your Thoughts and Feelings
♪ Study the Words of Latter-day Prophets and Apostles

♪ Look for Gospel Truths
♪ Listen to the Spirit
♪ Use Scripture Study Helps
♪ Share Insights
♪ Live by What You Learn

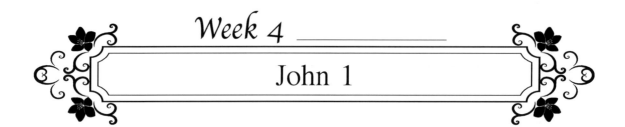

Week 4 _____

John 1

We Have Found the Messiah

Ideas to Improve Your Personal Scripture Study

♪ Look for Truths about Jesus Christ
♪ Look for Inspiring Words and Phrases
♪ Liken the Scriptures to Your life
♪ Ask Questions as You Study
♪ Record Your Thoughts and Feelings
♪ Study the Words of Latter-day Prophets and Apostles

♪ Look for Gospel Truths
♪ Listen to the Spirit
♪ Use Scripture Study Helps
♪ Share Insights
♪ Live by What You Learn

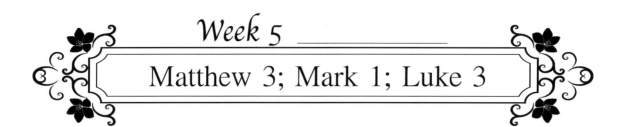

"Prepare Ye the Way of the Lord"

Ideas to Improve Your Personal Scripture Study

♪ Look for Truths about Jesus Christ
♪ Look for Inspiring Words and Phrases
♪ Liken the Scriptures to Your life
♪ Ask Questions as You Study
♪ Record Your Thoughts and Feelings
♪ Study the Words of Latter-day Prophets and Apostles

♪ Look for Gospel Truths
♪ Listen to the Spirit
♪ Use Scripture Study Helps
♪ Share Insights
♪ Live by What You Learn

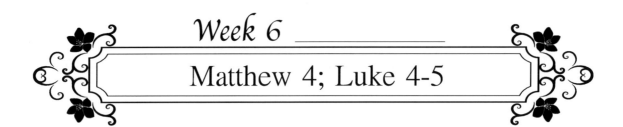

"The Spirit of the Lord Is upon Me"

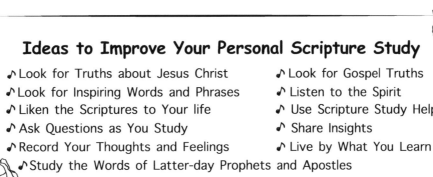

Ideas to Improve Your Personal Scripture Study

♪ Look for Truths about Jesus Christ
♪ Look for Inspiring Words and Phrases
♪ Liken the Scriptures to Your life
♪ Ask Questions as You Study
♪ Record Your Thoughts and Feelings

♪ Look for Gospel Truths
♪ Listen to the Spirit
♪ Use Scripture Study Helps
♪ Share Insights
♪ Live by What You Learn

♪ Study the Words of Latter-day Prophets and Apostles

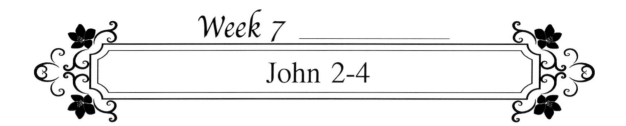

"Ye Must Be Born Again"

Ideas to Improve Your Personal Scripture Study

♪ Look for Truths about Jesus Christ
♪ Look for Inspiring Words and Phrases
♪ Liken the Scriptures to Your life
♪ Ask Questions as You Study
♪ Record Your Thoughts and Feelings

♪ Look for Gospel Truths
♪ Listen to the Spirit
♪ Use Scripture Study Helps
♪ Share Insights
♪ Live by What You Learn

♪ Study the Words of Latter-day Prophets and Apostles

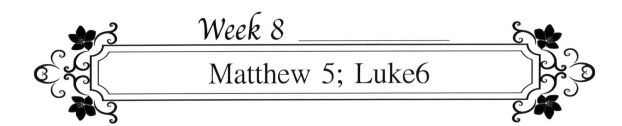

"Blessed Are Ye"

Ideas to Improve Your Personal Scripture Study

♪ Look for Truths about Jesus Christ   ♪ Look for Gospel Truths
♪ Look for Inspiring Words and Phrases   ♪ Listen to the Spirit
♪ Liken the Scriptures to Your life   ♪ Use Scripture Study Helps
♪ Ask Questions as You Study   ♪ Share Insights
♪ Record Your Thoughts and Feelings   ♪ Live by What You Learn
♪ Study the Words of Latter-day Prophets and Apostles

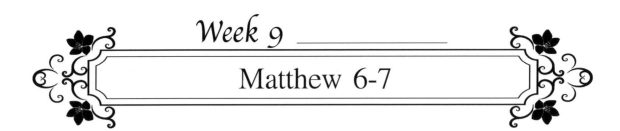

Ideas to Improve Your Personal Scripture Study

♪ Look for Truths about Jesus Christ
♪ Look for Inspiring Words and Phrases
♪ Liken the Scriptures to Your life
♪ Ask Questions as You Study
♪ Record Your Thoughts and Feelings

♪ Look for Gospel Truths
♪ Listen to the Spirit
♪ Use Scripture Study Helps
♪ Share Insights
♪ Live by What You Learn

♪ Study the Words of Latter-day Prophets and Apostles

Week 10

Matthew 8-9; Mark 2-5

"Thy Faith Hath Made Thee Whole"

Ideas to Improve Your Personal Scripture Study

♪ Look for Truths about Jesus Christ   ♪ Look for Gospel Truths

♪ Look for Inspiring Words and Phrases   ♪ Listen to the Spirit

♪ Liken the Scriptures to Your life   ♪ Use Scripture Study Helps

♪ Ask Questions as You Study   ♪ Share Insights

♪ Record Your Thoughts and Feelings   ♪ Live by What You Learn

♪ Study the Words of Latter-day Prophets and Apostles

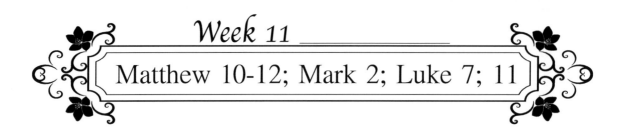

Ideas to Improve Your Personal Scripture Study

♪ Look for Truths about Jesus Christ
♪ Look for Inspiring Words and Phrases
♪ Liken the Scriptures to Your life
♪ Ask Questions as You Study
♪ Record Your Thoughts and Feelings
♪ Study the Words of Latter-day Prophets and Apostles

♪ Look for Gospel Truths
♪ Listen to the Spirit
♪ Use Scripture Study Helps
♪ Share Insights
♪ Live by What You Learn

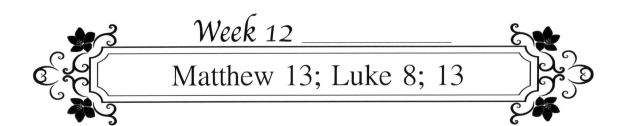

Matthew 13; Luke 8; 13

"Who Hath Ears to Hear, Let Him Hear"

Ideas to Improve Your Personal Scripture Study

♪ Look for Truths about Jesus Christ
♪ Look for Inspiring Words and Phrases
♪ Liken the Scriptures to Your life
♪ Ask Questions as You Study
♪ Record Your Thoughts and Feelings

♪ Look for Gospel Truths
♪ Listen to the Spirit
♪ Use Scripture Study Helps
♪ Share Insights
♪ Live by What You Learn

♪ Study the Words of Latter-day Prophets and Apostles

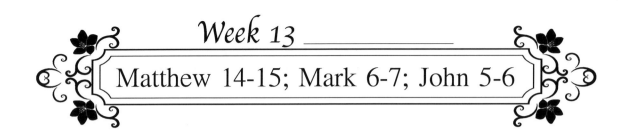

Week 13

Matthew 14-15; Mark 6-7; John 5-6

Ideas to Improve Your Personal Scripture Study

♪ Look for Truths about Jesus Christ   ♪ Look for Gospel Truths
♪ Look for Inspiring Words and Phrases   ♪ Listen to the Spirit
♪ Liken the Scriptures to Your life   ♪ Use Scripture Study Helps
♪ Ask Questions as You Study   ♪ Share Insights
♪ Record Your Thoughts and Feelings   ♪ Live by What You Learn
♪ Study the Words of Latter-day Prophets and Apostles

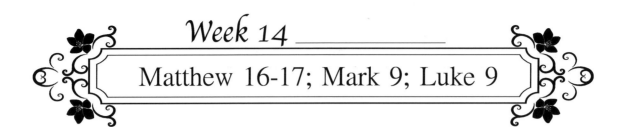

"Thou Art the Christ"

Ideas to Improve Your Personal Scripture Study

♪ Look for Truths about Jesus Christ
♪ Look for Inspiring Words and Phrases
♪ Liken the Scriptures to Your life
♪ Ask Questions as You Study
♪ Record Your Thoughts and Feelings
♪ Study the Words of Latter-day Prophets and Apostles

♪ Look for Gospel Truths
♪ Listen to the Spirit
♪ Use Scripture Study Helps
♪ Share Insights
♪ Live by What You Learn

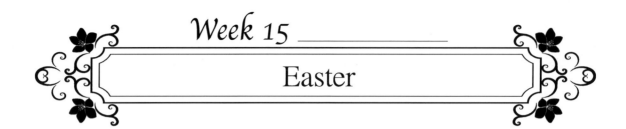

Easter

Ideas to Improve Your Personal Scripture Study

♪ Look for Truths about Jesus Christ   ♪ Look for Gospel Truths
♪ Look for Inspiring Words and Phrases   ♪ Listen to the Spirit
♪ Liken the Scriptures to Your life   ♪ Use Scripture Study Helps
♪ Ask Questions as You Study   ♪ Share Insights
♪ Record Your Thoughts and Feelings   ♪ Live by What You Learn
♪ Study the Words of Latter-day Prophets and Apostles

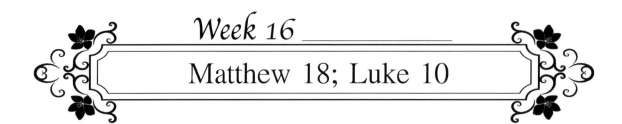

"What Shall I Do to Inherit Eternal Life?"

Ideas to Improve Your Personal Scripture Study

♪ Look for Truths about Jesus Christ
♪ Look for Inspiring Words and Phrases
♪ Liken the Scriptures to Your life
♪ Ask Questions as You Study
♪ Record Your Thoughts and Feelings
♪ Study the Words of Latter-day Prophets and Apostles

♪ Look for Gospel Truths
♪ Listen to the Spirit
♪ Use Scripture Study Helps
♪ Share Insights
♪ Live by What You Learn

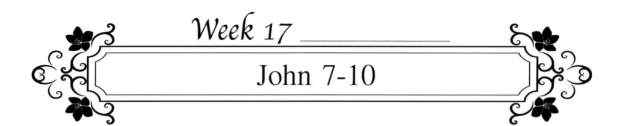

Week 17

John 7-10

"I Am the Good Shepherd"

Ideas to Improve Your Personal Scripture Study

♪ Look for Truths about Jesus Christ
♪ Look for Inspiring Words and Phrases
♪ Liken the Scriptures to Your life
♪ Ask Questions as You Study
♪ Record Your Thoughts and Feelings
♪ Study the Words of Latter-day Prophets and Apostles

♪ Look for Gospel Truths
♪ Listen to the Spirit
♪ Use Scripture Study Helps
♪ Share Insights
♪ Live by What You Learn

Week 18

Luke 12-17; John 11

Ideas to Improve Your Personal Scripture Study

♪ Look for Truths about Jesus Christ
♪ Look for Inspiring Words and Phrases
♪ Liken the Scriptures to Your life
♪ Ask Questions as You Study
♪ Record Your Thoughts and Feelings

♪ Look for Gospel Truths
♪ Listen to the Spirit
♪ Use Scripture Study Helps
♪ Share Insights
♪ Live by What You Learn

♪ Study the Words of Latter-day Prophets and Apostles

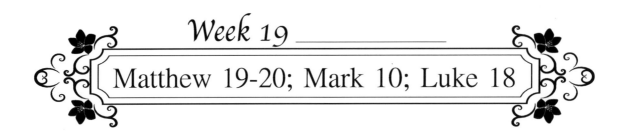

"What Lack I Yet?"

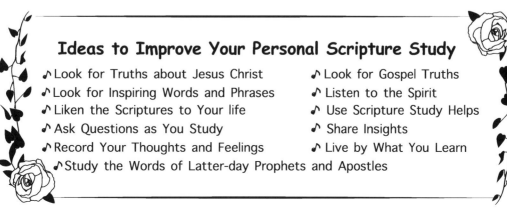

Ideas to Improve Your Personal Scripture Study

♪ Look for Truths about Jesus Christ
♪ Look for Inspiring Words and Phrases
♪ Liken the Scriptures to Your life
♪ Ask Questions as You Study
♪ Record Your Thoughts and Feelings

♪ Look for Gospel Truths
♪ Listen to the Spirit
♪ Use Scripture Study Helps
♪ Share Insights
♪ Live by What You Learn

♪ Study the Words of Latter-day Prophets and Apostles

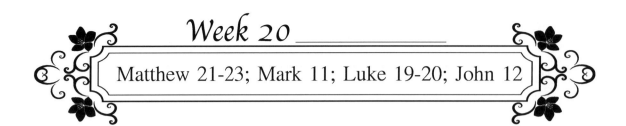

Week 20 _____

Matthew 21-23; Mark 11; Luke 19-20; John 12

"Behold, Thy King Cometh"

Ideas to Improve Your Personal Scripture Study

♪ Look for Truths about Jesus Christ
♪ Look for Inspiring Words and Phrases
♪ Liken the Scriptures to Your life
♪ Ask Questions as You Study
♪ Record Your Thoughts and Feelings
♪ Study the Words of Latter-day Prophets and Apostles

♪ Look for Gospel Truths
♪ Listen to the Spirit
♪ Use Scripture Study Helps
♪ Share Insights
♪ Live by What You Learn

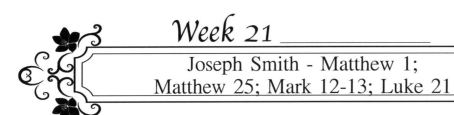

Week 21 _____

Joseph Smith - Matthew 1;
Matthew 25; Mark 12-13; Luke 21

"The Son of Man Shall Come"

Ideas to Improve Your Personal Scripture Study

♪ Look for Truths about Jesus Christ
♪ Look for Inspiring Words and Phrases
♪ Liken the Scriptures to Your life
♪ Ask Questions as You Study
♪ Record Your Thoughts and Feelings
♪ Look for Gospel Truths
♪ Listen to the Spirit
♪ Use Scripture Study Helps
♪ Share Insights
♪ Live by What You Learn
♪ Study the Words of Latter-day Prophets and Apostles

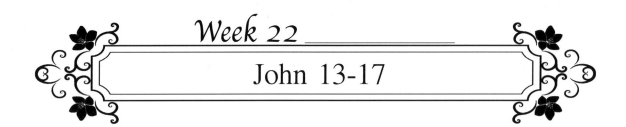

"Continue Ye in My Love"

Ideas to Improve Your Personal Scripture Study

♪ Look for Truths about Jesus Christ
♪ Look for Inspiring Words and Phrases
♪ Liken the Scriptures to Your life
♪ Ask Questions as You Study
♪ Record Your Thoughts and Feelings

♪ Look for Gospel Truths
♪ Listen to the Spirit
♪ Use Scripture Study Helps
♪ Share Insights
♪ Live by What You Learn

♪ Study the Words of Latter-day Prophets and Apostles

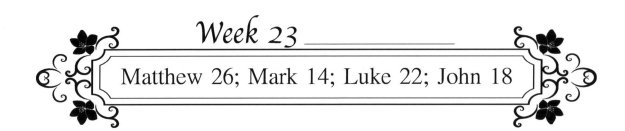

Week 23

Matthew 26; Mark 14; Luke 22; John 18

"Not as I Will, but as Thou Wilt"

Ideas to Improve Your Personal Scripture Study

♪ Look for Truths about Jesus Christ
♪ Look for Inspiring Words and Phrases
♪ Liken the Scriptures to Your life
♪ Ask Questions as You Study
♪ Record Your Thoughts and Feelings
♪ Study the Words of Latter-day Prophets and Apostles

♪ Look for Gospel Truths
♪ Listen to the Spirit
♪ Use Scripture Study Helps
♪ Share Insights
♪ Live by What You Learn

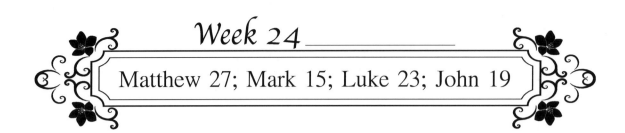

Week 24 _____

Matthew 27; Mark 15; Luke 23; John 19

"It Is Finished"

Ideas to Improve Your Personal Scripture Study

♪ Look for Truths about Jesus Christ ♪ Look for Gospel Truths
♪ Look for Inspiring Words and Phrases ♪ Listen to the Spirit
♪ Liken the Scriptures to Your life ♪ Use Scripture Study Helps
♪ Ask Questions as You Study ♪ Share Insights
♪ Record Your Thoughts and Feelings ♪ Live by What You Learn
♪ Study the Words of Latter-day Prophets and Apostles

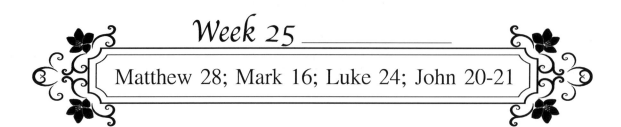

Week 25 _____

Matthew 28; Mark 16; Luke 24; John 20-21

"He is Risen"

Ideas to Improve Your Personal Scripture Study

♪ Look for Truths about Jesus Christ
♪ Look for Inspiring Words and Phrases
♪ Liken the Scriptures to Your life
♪ Ask Questions as You Study
♪ Record Your Thoughts and Feelings

♪ Look for Gospel Truths
♪ Listen to the Spirit
♪ Use Scripture Study Helps
♪ Share Insights
♪ Live by What You Learn

♪ Study the Words of Latter-day Prophets and Apostles

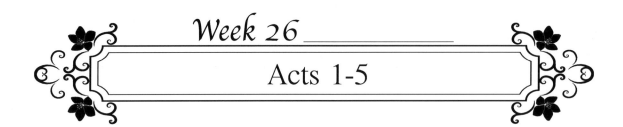

"Ye Shall Be Witnesses unto Me"

Ideas to Improve Your Personal Scripture Study

♪ Look for Truths about Jesus Christ
♪ Look for Inspiring Words and Phrases
♪ Liken the Scriptures to Your life
♪ Ask Questions as You Study
♪ Record Your Thoughts and Feelings
♪ Study the Words of Latter-day Prophets and Apostles

♪ Look for Gospel Truths
♪ Listen to the Spirit
♪ Use Scripture Study Helps
♪ Share Insights
♪ Live by What You Learn

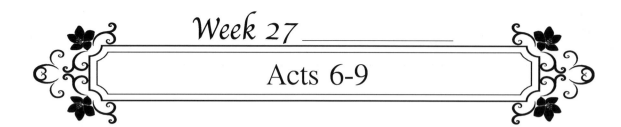

"What Wilt Thou Have Me to Do?"

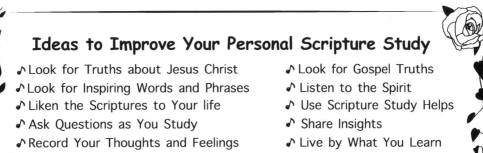

Ideas to Improve Your Personal Scripture Study

♪ Look for Truths about Jesus Christ
♪ Look for Inspiring Words and Phrases
♪ Liken the Scriptures to Your life
♪ Ask Questions as You Study
♪ Record Your Thoughts and Feelings
♪ Look for Gospel Truths
♪ Listen to the Spirit
♪ Use Scripture Study Helps
♪ Share Insights
♪ Live by What You Learn
♪ Study the Words of Latter-day Prophets and Apostles

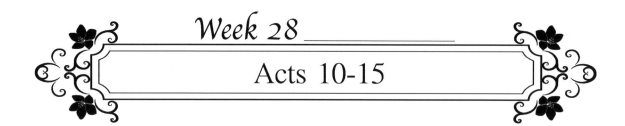

Week 28

Acts 10-15

"The Word of God Grew and Multiplied"

Ideas to Improve Your Personal Scripture Study

♪ Look for Truths about Jesus Christ
♪ Look for Inspiring Words and Phrases
♪ Liken the Scriptures to Your life
♪ Ask Questions as You Study
♪ Record Your Thoughts and Feelings
♪ Study the Words of Latter-day Prophets and Apostles

♪ Look for Gospel Truths
♪ Listen to the Spirit
♪ Use Scripture Study Helps
♪ Share Insights
♪ Live by What You Learn

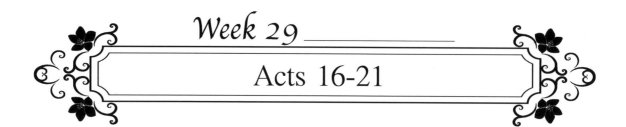

Week 29 _____

Acts 16-21

Ideas to Improve Your Personal Scripture Study

♪ Look for Truths about Jesus Christ
♪ Look for Inspiring Words and Phrases
♪ Liken the Scriptures to Your life
♪ Ask Questions as You Study
♪ Record Your Thoughts and Feelings

♪ Look for Gospel Truths
♪ Listen to the Spirit
♪ Use Scripture Study Helps
♪ Share Insights
♪ Live by What You Learn

♪ Study the Words of Latter-day Prophets and Apostles

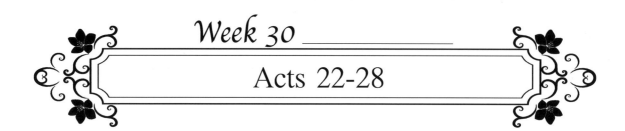

Week 30

Acts 22-28

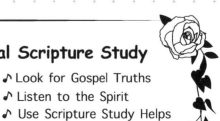

Ideas to Improve Your Personal Scripture Study

♪ Look for Truths about Jesus Christ   ♪ Look for Gospel Truths
♪ Look for Inspiring Words and Phrases   ♪ Listen to the Spirit
♪ Liken the Scriptures to Your life   ♪ Use Scripture Study Helps
♪ Ask Questions as You Study   ♪ Share Insights
♪ Record Your Thoughts and Feelings   ♪ Live by What You Learn
♪ Study the Words of Latter-day Prophets and Apostles

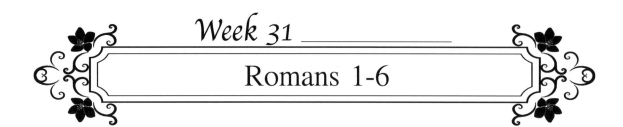

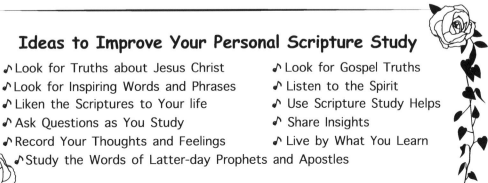

Ideas to Improve Your Personal Scripture Study

♪ Look for Truths about Jesus Christ
♪ Look for Inspiring Words and Phrases
♪ Liken the Scriptures to Your life
♪ Ask Questions as You Study
♪ Record Your Thoughts and Feelings
♪ Study the Words of Latter-day Prophets and Apostles

♪ Look for Gospel Truths
♪ Listen to the Spirit
♪ Use Scripture Study Helps
♪ Share Insights
♪ Live by What You Learn

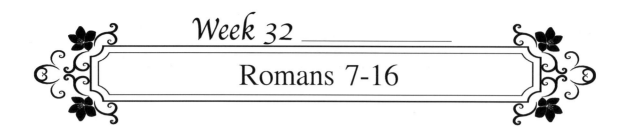

Week 32 _____

Romans 7-16

"Overcome Evil with Good"

Ideas to Improve Your Personal Scripture Study

♪ Look for Truths about Jesus Christ
♪ Look for Inspiring Words and Phrases
♪ Liken the Scriptures to Your life
♪ Ask Questions as You Study
♪ Record Your Thoughts and Feelings
♪ Study the Words of Latter-day Prophets and Apostles

♪ Look for Gospel Truths
♪ Listen to the Spirit
♪ Use Scripture Study Helps
♪ Share Insights
♪ Live by What You Learn

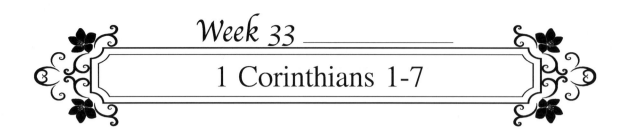

"Be Perfectly Joined Together"

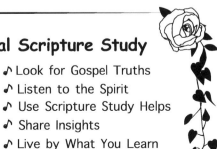

Ideas to Improve Your Personal Scripture Study

♪ Look for Truths about Jesus Christ
♪ Look for Inspiring Words and Phrases
♪ Liken the Scriptures to Your life
♪ Ask Questions as You Study
♪ Record Your Thoughts and Feelings
♪ Study the Words of Latter-day Prophets and Apostles

♪ Look for Gospel Truths
♪ Listen to the Spirit
♪ Use Scripture Study Helps
♪ Share Insights
♪ Live by What You Learn

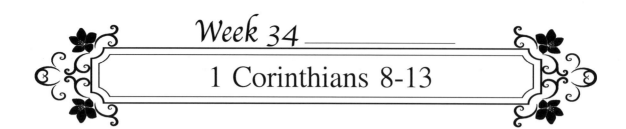

Week 34

1 Corinthians 8-13

Ideas to Improve Your Personal Scripture Study

♪ Look for Truths about Jesus Christ
♪ Look for Inspiring Words and Phrases
♪ Liken the Scriptures to Your life
♪ Ask Questions as You Study
♪ Record Your Thoughts and Feelings

♪ Look for Gospel Truths
♪ Listen to the Spirit
♪ Use Scripture Study Helps
♪ Share Insights
♪ Live by What You Learn

♪ Study the Words of Latter-day Prophets and Apostles

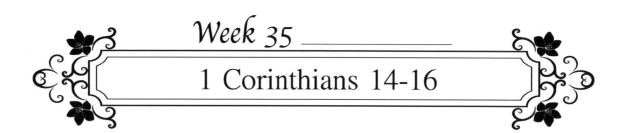

Week 35 _____

1 Corinthians 14-16

Ideas to Improve Your Personal Scripture Study

♪ Look for Truths about Jesus Christ
♪ Look for Gospel Truths
♪ Look for Inspiring Words and Phrases
♪ Listen to the Spirit
♪ Liken the Scriptures to Your life
♪ Use Scripture Study Helps
♪ Ask Questions as You Study
♪ Share Insights
♪ Record Your Thoughts and Feelings
♪ Live by What You Learn
♪ Study the Words of Latter-day Prophets and Apostles

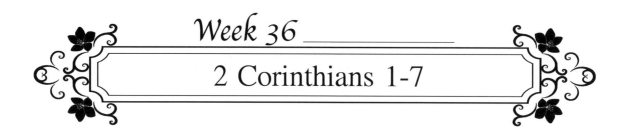

Week 36

2 Corinthians 1-7

Ideas to Improve Your Personal Scripture Study

♪ Look for Truths about Jesus Christ
♪ Look for Inspiring Words and Phrases
♪ Liken the Scriptures to Your life
♪ Ask Questions as You Study
♪ Record Your Thoughts and Feelings
♪ Look for Gospel Truths
♪ Listen to the Spirit
♪ Use Scripture Study Helps
♪ Share Insights
♪ Live by What You Learn
♪ Study the Words of Latter-day Prophets and Apostles

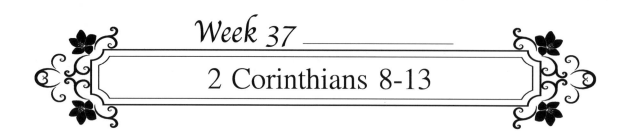

"God Loveth a Cheerful Giver"

Ideas to Improve Your Personal Scripture Study

♪ Look for Truths about Jesus Christ
♪ Look for Inspiring Words and Phrases
♪ Liken the Scriptures to Your life
♪ Ask Questions as You Study
♪ Record Your Thoughts and Feelings
♪ Study the Words of Latter-day Prophets and Apostles

♪ Look for Gospel Truths
♪ Listen to the Spirit
♪ Use Scripture Study Helps
♪ Share Insights
♪ Live by What You Learn

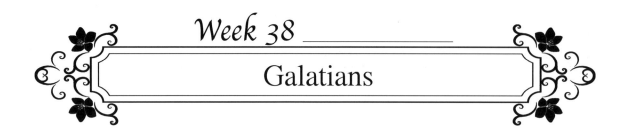

Galatians

"Walk in the Spirit"

Ideas to Improve Your Personal Scripture Study

♪ Look for Truths about Jesus Christ

♪ Look for Inspiring Words and Phrases

♪ Liken the Scriptures to Your life

♪ Ask Questions as You Study

♪ Record Your Thoughts and Feelings

♪ Look for Gospel Truths

♪ Listen to the Spirit

♪ Use Scripture Study Helps

♪ Share Insights

♪ Live by What You Learn

♪ Study the Words of Latter-day Prophets and Apostles

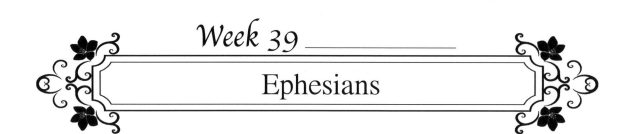

Week 39 _____

Ephesians

"For the Perfecting of the Saints"

Ideas to Improve Your Personal Scripture Study

♪ Look for Truths about Jesus Christ
♪ Look for Inspiring Words and Phrases
♪ Liken the Scriptures to Your life
♪ Ask Questions as You Study
♪ Record Your Thoughts and Feelings
♪ Study the Words of Latter-day Prophets and Apostles

♪ Look for Gospel Truths
♪ Listen to the Spirit
♪ Use Scripture Study Helps
♪ Share Insights
♪ Live by What You Learn

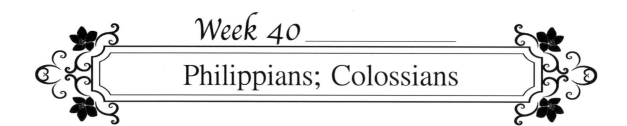

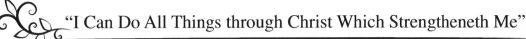

"I Can Do All Things through Christ Which Strengtheneth Me"

Ideas to Improve Your Personal Scripture Study

♪ Look for Truths about Jesus Christ
♪ Look for Inspiring Words and Phrases
♪ Liken the Scriptures to Your life
♪ Ask Questions as You Study
♪ Record Your Thoughts and Feelings

♪ Look for Gospel Truths
♪ Listen to the Spirit
♪ Use Scripture Study Helps
♪ Share Insights
♪ Live by What You Learn

♪ Study the Words of Latter-day Prophets and Apostles

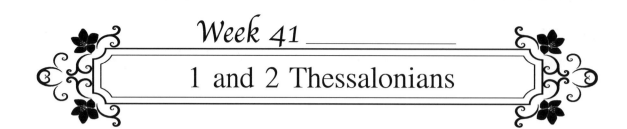

Ideas to Improve Your Personal Scripture Study

♪ Look for Truths about Jesus Christ

♪ Look for Inspiring Words and Phrases

♪ Liken the Scriptures to Your life

♪ Ask Questions as You Study

♪ Record Your Thoughts and Feelings

♪ Look for Gospel Truths

♪ Listen to the Spirit

♪ Use Scripture Study Helps

♪ Share Insights

♪ Live by What You Learn

♪ Study the Words of Latter-day Prophets and Apostles

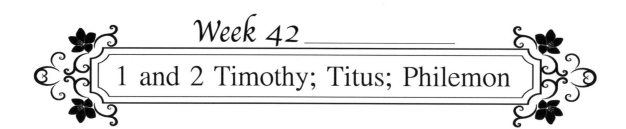

Week 42

1 and 2 Timothy; Titus; Philemon

"Be Thou an Example of the Believers"

Ideas to Improve Your Personal Scripture Study

♪ Look for Truths about Jesus Christ
♪ Look for Inspiring Words and Phrases
♪ Liken the Scriptures to Your life
♪ Ask Questions as You Study
♪ Record Your Thoughts and Feelings
♪ Study the Words of Latter-day Prophets and Apostles

♪ Look for Gospel Truths
♪ Listen to the Spirit
♪ Use Scripture Study Helps
♪ Share Insights
♪ Live by What You Learn

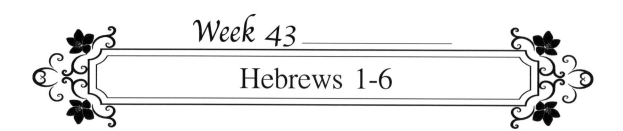

Week 43

Hebrews 1-6

Ideas to Improve Your Personal Scripture Study

♪ Look for Truths about Jesus Christ
♪ Look for Inspiring Words and Phrases
♪ Liken the Scriptures to Your life
♪ Ask Questions as You Study
♪ Record Your Thoughts and Feelings
♪ Study the Words of Latter-day Prophets and Apostles

♪ Look for Gospel Truths
♪ Listen to the Spirit
♪ Use Scripture Study Helps
♪ Share Insights
♪ Live by What You Learn

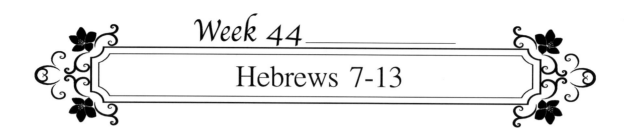

Week 44

Hebrews 7-13

"An High Priest of Good Things to Come"

Ideas to Improve Your Personal Scripture Study

♪ Look for Truths about Jesus Christ
♪ Look for Inspiring Words and Phrases
♪ Liken the Scriptures to Your life
♪ Ask Questions as You Study
♪ Record Your Thoughts and Feelings
♪ Study the Words of Latter-day Prophets and Apostles

♪ Look for Gospel Truths
♪ Listen to the Spirit
♪ Use Scripture Study Helps
♪ Share Insights
♪ Live by What You Learn

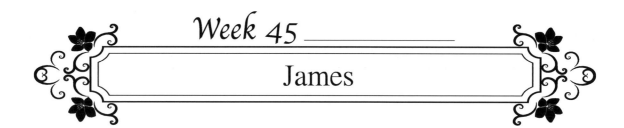

James

"Be Ye Doers of the Word, and Not Hearers Only"

Ideas to Improve Your Personal Scripture Study

♪ Look for Truths about Jesus Christ
♪ Look for Inspiring Words and Phrases
♪ Liken the Scriptures to Your life
♪ Ask Questions as You Study
♪ Record Your Thoughts and Feelings
♪ Study the Words of Latter-day Prophets and Apostles

♪ Look for Gospel Truths
♪ Listen to the Spirit
♪ Use Scripture Study Helps
♪ Share Insights
♪ Live by What You Learn

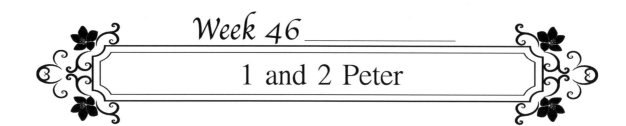

Week 46

1 and 2 Peter

Ideas to Improve Your Personal Scripture Study

♪ Look for Truths about Jesus Christ
♪ Look for Inspiring Words and Phrases
♪ Liken the Scriptures to Your life
♪ Ask Questions as You Study
♪ Record Your Thoughts and Feelings

♪ Look for Gospel Truths
♪ Listen to the Spirit
♪ Use Scripture Study Helps
♪ Share Insights
♪ Live by What You Learn

♪ Study the Words of Latter-day Prophets and Apostles

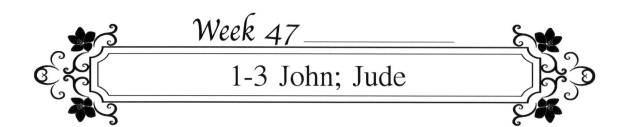

1-3 John; Jude

"God is Love"

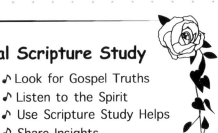

Ideas to Improve Your Personal Scripture Study

♪ Look for Truths about Jesus Christ   ♪ Look for Gospel Truths
♪ Look for Inspiring Words and Phrases   ♪ Listen to the Spirit
♪ Liken the Scriptures to Your life   ♪ Use Scripture Study Helps
♪ Ask Questions as You Study   ♪ Share Insights
♪ Record Your Thoughts and Feelings   ♪ Live by What You Learn
♪ Study the Words of Latter-day Prophets and Apostles

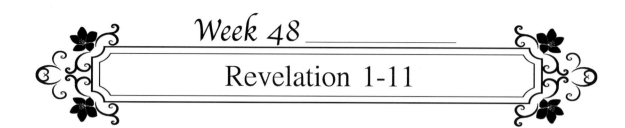

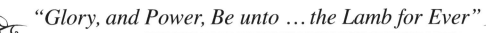

Ideas to Improve Your Personal Scripture Study

♪ Look for Truths about Jesus Christ   ♪ Look for Gospel Truths
♪ Look for Inspiring Words and Phrases   ♪ Listen to the Spirit
♪ Liken the Scriptures to Your life   ♪ Use Scripture Study Helps
♪ Ask Questions as You Study   ♪ Share Insights
♪ Record Your Thoughts and Feelings   ♪ Live by What You Learn
♪ Study the Words of Latter-day Prophets and Apostles

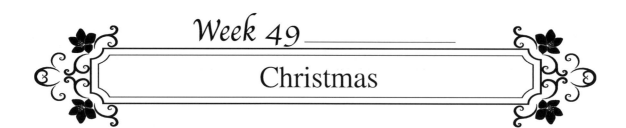

Ideas to Improve Your Personal Scripture Study

♪ Look for Truths about Jesus Christ
♪ Look for Inspiring Words and Phrases
♪ Liken the Scriptures to Your life
♪ Ask Questions as You Study
♪ Record Your Thoughts and Feelings
♪ Study the Words of Latter-day Prophets and Apostles

♪ Look for Gospel Truths
♪ Listen to the Spirit
♪ Use Scripture Study Helps
♪ Share Insights
♪ Live by What You Learn

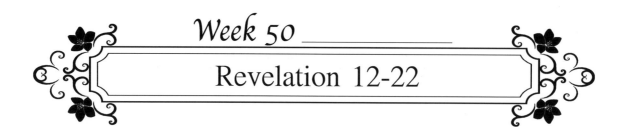

Ideas to Improve Your Personal Scripture Study

♪ Look for Truths about Jesus Christ
♪ Look for Inspiring Words and Phrases
♪ Liken the Scriptures to Your life
♪ Ask Questions as You Study
♪ Record Your Thoughts and Feelings
♪ Study the Words of Latter-day Prophets and Apostles

♪ Look for Gospel Truths
♪ Listen to the Spirit
♪ Use Scripture Study Helps
♪ Share Insights
♪ Live by What You Learn

Made in the USA
San Bernardino, CA
22 December 2018